In-Between

eight gender-neutral one-act plays

between life and death

by Niki J. Borger

Library of Congress Control Number: 2026909947
ISBN (Print): 979-8-9956888-0-8
ISBN (eBook): 979-8-9956888-1-5

First Edition 2026

Burbank, California

Published by Idle Hour Press.
Printed on demand in the country of purchase.

Interior set in Lato and Cinzel.
Edited by Elizabeth Joyce A.

www.nikijborger.com

TO MY PARENTS

WHO ENABLED ME TO FOLLOW THIS PATH

AND NOW WATCH ME WALK IT

FROM THE OTHER SIDE.

NOTES ON PRODUCTION

As an artist, I believe strongly in the power of co-creation and open creativity. I have provided the general framework, the rules of the world, the dialogue, and the story arcs for each character. Beyond that, please feel free to make these stories your own. Experiment. Be bold. Let your individuality flow through these characters and narratives. Allow them to become a shared creation between all of us, so that each time they are staged, they feel fresh, authentic, and full of life.

That said, please remain respectful and obtain the necessary rights prior to production. Rights are required for any public performance—professional, educational, or amateur—including staged readings. They can be obtained at www.nikijborger.com/plays. If you have any questions or concerns, you are welcome to reach out at any time.

The plays in this collection may be produced individually or as a full-length production. If producing the complete set, it should be presented under the title *In-Between*. The plays should be performed in the following order:

1. The Invention of Death

2. Ninety Seven Beats
3. The Helper's Hand
4. Crash / Kill
– Intermission –
5. Teddy Bears and Scented Candles
6. Quarterlife Check-Up
7. Joey and Jace
8. Honey, I'm Leaving

Additionally, I'd suggest the following:

Adjust any lines that imply an incorrect gender, age, or other denomination, as needed.

Keep sets minimal to reduce the need for scene changes.

Use music during transitions to help establish the time period, location, and tone of the upcoming play.

If the cast size allows, consider having the same actors portray characters across different lifetimes to support the themes of reincarnation and karma present throughout the work. If the production includes more than the 12 actors required, roles may be distributed across plays, but continuity should still be maintained through costume, accent, style, attitude, and overall physical and emotional presence. With a cast of 12, the roles should be covered as follows:

actor	gender	The Invention of Death	Ninety Seven Beats (1987)	The Helper's Hand	Crash / Kill (1989)	Teddy Bears and Scented Candles (1991)	Quarter-life Check-Up (2020)	Joey and Jace (2021)	Honey, I'm leaving (2026)
1		Anh				Voice			
2		Ohm							
3			Micah					Jace	
4			Ariel	Ariel					
5	(f)		Abbie/ Abigail						Gail/ Abigail
6			Doctor			Dad		(Doctor)	Jo

actor	gender	The Invention of Death	Ninety Seven Beats (1987)	The Helper's Hand	Crash / Kill (1989)	Teddy Bears and Scented Candles (1991)	Quarter-life Check-Up (2020)	Joey and Jace (2021)	Honey, I'm leaving (2026)
7					Riley			Joey	
8				Rib	Rib				
9		(Human)			Casey	Casey		(Nurse)	
10	(f)					Jen			Terry
11				Cricket			Cricket		
12	f		(Nurse)				Sai	Sai	

Notes from the Author

Thank you for picking up this book and taking the time to read my thoughts. I care deeply about its stories, its themes, and especially its world, for two reasons.

First, over the course of the past eight years, I became intimately familiar with death and the subjects surrounding it. As I lost my mother, my stepfather, my father, and all of my grandparents, death, its meaning, and its purpose became something I had to confront in order to stay grounded through the process.

You may not agree with the perspectives presented in these stories. You may feel that my views are unproven or ultimately unprovable and you would be right. However, this way of understanding life has brought me considerable comfort, freedom from anxiety, and, ultimately, peace with what has occurred. I sincerely hope it may offer something similar to you.

Second, aside from the experience of childbirth, which is biologically limited to women (for now), I no longer believe that stories and human experiences should be assigned to a specific gender at the point of creation. Who has the authority to define that "this is a man's story" or "this is a nonbinary person's story"? In my view, only the actor can determine whether they connect with a story or not. The same applies to race, sexual orientation, and other superficial distinctions we often use to separate ourselves and divide our communities.

I absolutely do not deny that harmful injustices have occurred in the past, and continue to occur today, affecting certain groups worse than others. Those stories deserve to be told with the highest level of historical and sociological accuracy, honesty, care, and integrity.

However, in works without specific historical or sociological context, such as this one, the question of representation is best determined at the individual level. As a director, you decide whether a story resonates with your vision. As an actor, you decide whether you can and wish to inhabit a character. No external label—whether gender, race, sexual orientation, or any other—should prevent you from telling the stories you feel compelled to tell.

I have done my best to reflect this philosophy in my writing, which may occasionally result in phrasing that feels uneven or imperfect. I ask for your understanding in that regard.

Whoever you are, if these stories resonate with you, I would be honored for you to bring them to life freely, without limitation, expectation, or anything that might stand in the way of your authentic expression. Thank you <3

TABLE OF CONTENTS

Notes on Production............IV

Notes from the Author............VIII

The Invention of Death............12

Ninety Seven Beats............26

The Helper's Hand............39

Crash / Kill............50

Teddy Bears and Scented Candles............62

Quarterlife Check-Up............78

Joey and Jace............89

Honey, I'm leaving............102

THE INVENTION OF DEATH

by Niki J. Borger

Overview
A 15-minute comedy
For 3 actors of any gender

Synopsis
While creating the human experience, the divine
parents Ohm and Anh decide to add a fail-safe.

Characters
ANH [aːn]   – divine creator; feminine energy
OHM [oʊm] – divine creator; masculine energy
HUMAN   – any age, preferably younger

Setting
Before space and time, an undefined place at the
heart of creation.

Scene 1

*Lights up on an empty space of pure
potential. From off stage, the sounds of
thousands of children and their activities
can be heard. Their parents, ANH and OHM,
do their best to mitigate the chaos.*

ANH. *(o.s.)* Careful, love. Ohmo just made that
         cosmic web.
OHM. *(o.s.)* Well done, honey
ANH. *(o.s.)* Why don't you just put it up there
OHM. *(o.s.)* Gaia, Cronos, stop teasing your
         younger siblings.
ANH. *(o.s.)* Yes, that's very good, love
OHM. *(o.s.)* Why don't you play with this one?
ANH. *(o.s.)* Slowly, Orion!
OHM. *(o.s.)* Yes, I'll be right back–
ANH. *(o.s.)* Just one–

> *Both Anh and Ohm enter the stage and*
> *quickly shut the doors behind them,*
> *drowning out the noise from outside.*

> *Anh sinks down onto something to sit. Ohm*
> *joins Anh.*

OHM. I am exhausted!

> *Anh takes a deep breath before answering.*

ANH. Tell me about it.

> *Ohm puts their arm around Anh.*

OHM. Want me to help you relax?

> *Anh looks at Ohm in disbelief, then pushes*
> *Ohm away.*

ANH. You helping me relax is what got us into this
         chaos!
OHM. Ah.
ANH. Seven thousand five hundred thirty-three
         times.
OHM. Right.
ANH. And now we have seven thousand five
         hundred thirty-three tiny gods walking
         around doing whatever they want.

         *From off stage, a massive shattering noise is
         heard.*

ANH. I think that was your new cosmic web.

         *Ohm jumps up and looks out through the
         door. Then they close it again, slightly
         defeated.*

OHM. I think you're right.

         Ohm rejoins Anh.

ANH. Ohm.
OHM. Anh?
ANH. We can't keep doing this.
OHM. Parenting?
ANH. Having more children...
OHM. Ah.

         A realization dawns.

OHM. But I want to make love to my love!
ANH. Not anymore.
OHM. At least canoodling?
ANH. No.
OHM. A kiss?
ANH. No.
OHM. Just a little hug?
ANH. Absolutely not.
OHM. For how long?

Anh throws Ohm a glance.

OHM. ...shit.

Lights down.

Scene 2

Lights up on the same setting. A HUMAN now stands between Anh and Ohm. Dressed in a white tunic, their eyes are almost closed. They are immobile, like a figurine.

ANH. Are you out of your mind?
OHM. I think it's brilliant!
ANH. You want to put our little souls in this?!
OHM. Yes! It'll keep them occupied, and you and I, we get a break. Like a game!

*Ohm puts their arm around Anh, who
pushes them away almost immediately. Anh
begins examining the Human.*

ANH. And what can this vessel do?
OHM. Here, let me show you.

Ohm rushes to the door and calls out.

OHM. Ara, can you come here?

Ohm lets an invisible Ara pass.

OHM. *(to Ara)* Do me a favor and inhabit this body
      for a moment, okay?

*The Human slowly comes to life. They look
around, discovering their arms and legs, and
begin moving. At first, they are clumsy, but
gradually gain coordination. Ohm and Anh
observe.*

OHM. I call it: a human. And it can do all sorts of
      things.
ANH. Like what?
OHM. It can create beautiful things like music,
      smart things like machines, loving things like
      friendships. Here, let me show you.

*Ohm pulls a set of wooden sticks (or
something similarly simple) out of nowhere
and hands them to the Human, who begins*

to play with them like a two-year-old:
clumsily, noisily, and messily.

ANH. I'm not impressed.
OHM. Patience.
ANH. So each soul would get its own human body?
OHM. Correct.

The Human is now throwing sticks left and
right, making a loud, chaotic mess.

ANH. I can't see how this will improve anything
        here.
OHM. Oh. We'll send them away to a place made
        for humans. I call it Earth.
ANH. Like a playground?
OHM. Exactly. It will abide by the laws of physics,
        time and space, which will keep them from
        causing too much damage.
ANH. Space? I don't like the sound of that word.
OHM. Space lets things be apart.
ANH. So you want to separate them?
OHM. Yes.
ANH. And if they can't find one another, they'll be
        all alone?

The Human begins building something.

OHM. Never for long, because there will also be
        time.
ANH. What is time?
OHM. Time lets things happen one after another.

ANH. What if they do something and then want to
          change it?
OHM. …Well, I'm afraid there is no going back in
          time.
ANH. So you will force them to live with regret?
OHM. No

          *The Human's building collapses. They are
          upset.*

ANH. And we won't be there to console them,
          because you want our children to be far
          away from us. Oh, honey…

          *Anh moves to hug the Human, but the
          Human does not react at all.*

ANH. What's happening?
OHM. Ara can't see you.
ANH. What?
OHM. Well, they can't know that we exist, can
          they?

          The Human starts again.

ANH. WHAT?!
OHM. Or they'd want to be back all the time. And if
          they're back here, then the whole
          experiment would be pointless.
ANH. They would not know about their home,
          their family, the love that created them?!
OHM. They can't miss what they can't remember…

ANH. This is a cruel idea!

Ohm does not answer.

ANH. And you call yourself a parent.

Ohm is at a loss for words.

OHM. I didn't mean to upset you, my love.

Anh does not respond.

OHM. I just hate seeing you burned out like this.

*Ohm walks up to Anh but maintains a
respectful distance.*

ANH. As if this was about me...
OHM. Well, it's about all of us.

Anh takes a moment before admitting

ANH. I'd like a little more peace and quiet.

*From outside the room, another very loud
shattering sound can be heard. Both Anh
and Ohm look toward the door.*

OHM. That was probably the other cosmic web I
     made...

*The Human has finished their first ever
creation. Anh and Ohm notice it.*

ANH. It's beautiful.
OHM. Look how proud it is.

Anh and Ohm both grow a little emotional.

ANH. Right. Let's wrap this up.
OHM. Already?
ANH. Absolutely.
OHM. It hasn't even
ANH. Now!
OHM. Okay. *(in an almighty, divine voice)* Ara, you
       can come out now.

*The Human clearly hears the voice but does
not know where it is coming from.*

OHM. *(almighty, divine voice)* Ara, it's me. Time to
       leave the human and come out.

The Human shakes its head.

OHM. *(to Anh)* Is that a no?
ANH. *(almighty, divine voice to Ara)* Honey, don't
       be ridiculous. It's time to come home.

*The Human shakes its head again. They sit
down with their creation and begin
rebuilding it into something better.*

OHM. Seems like it's enjoying it.
ANH. *(even more divine voice)* Ara, dear, it's your
          Anha. Time to come home.

          *The Human ignores them and continues
          building.*

ANH. *(to Ohm)* Great. What now?
OHM. That is a good question...
ANH. How are we getting Ara out?

          *Ohm begins looking for something that
          could help, then looks at the Human for any
          hints.*

OHM. I haven't thought this far, okay...
ANH. Typical.
OHM. Not helping.
ANH. They won't want to leave while they're
          having fun.
OHM. Right.
ANH. You should've thought of that before putting
          our child in there.
OHM. You didn't think of it either!
ANH. It's not my creation!
OHM. And yours are always perfect?
ANH. Excuse me! I have created seven thousand
          five hundred and thirty-three tiny little
          replicas of ourselves, while you were just
OHM. You're right, you're right, sorry–

*Ohm moves closer to Anh in an attempt to
console, but Anh is not receptive.*

OHM. I helped create them.
ANH. Did you really?!
OHM. For a... hot... moment...

*The Human injures itself while playing and
begins to cry. Both parents notice
immediately.*

ANH. What's happening?
OHM. It must have hurt itself somehow...
ANH. Hurt? What's that?
OHM. Hurt, pain. A feeling of severe discomfort
        that leads to recovery and growth. It's a
        necessary part of the human experience so
        they evolve.

The Human cries more and more.

ANH. Do something about it!
OHM. There's nothing we can really do...
ANH. You're joking!
OHM. It'll start healing on its own soon, and it'll be
        fine!
ANH. We just stand here and watch?!
OHM. Not a good idea, you're right. Uhm...
        (attempting divine voice) Ara, just come out.
        You can let this body go.

The Human cries harder than ever.

ANH. *(divine voice)* Ara, dear, come out and it'll be
       over.
OHM. *(divine voice)* Come on, Ara. Just come out.
ANH. I don't think it hears us any more. What have
       you done?!
OHM. *(to themselves)* Interesting! I wonder, why...
ANH. Ohm, our child needs a way back home!
OHM. You're right. I just don't know how.

> *Ohm desperately looks for something to
> help.*

ANH. You should have thought of this!
OHM. Not helping, alright?! *(mightiest voice ever)*
       Ara? ARA!
ANH. *(inspiration strikes)* I have an idea.
OHM. Share it, will you?!
ANH. It's simple: our little souls are eternal. They
       live forever. Right? So... we just terminate
       the vessel.
OHM. Oh. OH!
ANH. This isn't your only prototype, is it?
OHM. No, of course not. I made a bunch of
       different models.
ANH. Good.

> *Anh looks around, then picks up one of the
> wooden sticks.*

ANH. Where?
OHM. Uhm... there's a weak spot right there.

*Ohm indicates the Human's neck. The
Human's crying begins to lessen as Anh
approaches, carefully but clearly torn. Anh
does not want to do this but sees no other
option.*

OHM. You sure it won't do anything to Ara?
ANH. You tell me, you created the vessel!
OHM. Right. I think it'll be fine.
ANH. You think?!
OHM. It should be fine.
ANH. "Should" is not enough. This is our child!

Anh stops in their tracks.

ANH. I can't do it. You do it!
OHM. What? No.
ANH. You do it. You got us into this, now get us
        out!
OHM. I can't… what if we just wait it out?
ANH. OHM!

*The Human stops crying and examines the
injury, which has begun to heal. For a
moment, there is silence. Then the Human
resumes playing, peacefully and with
greater skill than before.*

OHM. Look, it's over already.
ANH. But we still don't have Ara back.
OHM. How about I create a natural way something
        in their nature, their physique, or their

    environment that, after some time, will
    bring them back.
ANH. A fail-safe. Whatever happens, they will
    always come back home eventually.
OHM. Precisely.
ANH. Fine. Just get Ara back.
OHM. I will.

Ohm makes a mental note.

OHM. Create Death. What else do we need?
ANH. I still don't like the idea of them being alone.
OHM. If you can make divine helpers, I will send
    them to the right places. *(mental note)*
    Assign Angels. Anything else?
ANH. Make sure nothing can happen to their souls,
    ever.
OHM. You got it.

*Ohm pulls Anh into a hug, and Anh finally
does not resist. At that very moment,
another massive noise can be heard from
outside.*

ANH. What do you think that was?
OHM. Who cares. *(pulls Anh closer)* Now… where
    were we?

End of Play.

Ninety Seven Beats

by Niki J. Borger

Overview
A 15-minute drama
for 5 actors (1 female and 4 any gender)

Synopsis
When Micah's heart is down to its final beats, they
bargain for more time with the woman they love.

Characters
MICAH   – 20s to 30s
ARIEL   – any age
ABBIE (ABIGAIL)   – 20s to 30s, female, Micah's
                            wife
DOCTOR   – 30s to 60s
NURSE   – 20s to 60s

Setting
1987. A hospital room. A single hospital bed is
centered in the space. A heartbeat monitor is
positioned behind it. A chair sits to one side.

Notes
All characters except Abbie may be played by
actors of any gender. Pronouns and lines should be
adjusted accordingly.

"On" may be indicated by a light originating from above the audience.
Scene 3 takes place in complete darkness. Alternatively, sound effects and dialogue for this scene may be prerecorded, though a live performance will likely create a more vivid audience experience.
Once the performance has been staged, any lines indicating the number of heartbeats remaining should be adjusted to reflect the actual count.

Original Premiere
Ninety Seven Beats premiered on June 1, 2025, at the 2025 Extravaganza One-Act Fest, directed by Wolfgang Bodison.

Original Cast
MICAH   – Dylan Marusich
ARIEL   – Niki J. Borger
ABBIE   – Erin Hadfield
DOCTOR   – Megan Corse
NURSE   – Rebecca Tarabocchia

Scene 1

Lights up on a hospital room. A NURSE pushes a hospital bed into the room. MICAH lies motionless in it. The nurse places a heartbeat monitor beside Micah's bed and attaches the cables. The nurse draws some blood. The steady beeping of the heartbeat monitor can be heard.

ABBIE enters in a rush. She checks on Micah, waits, prays. The DOCTOR enters.

DOCTOR. Mrs. Donahue? I'm Doctor Whitney. Unfortunately, Micah has severe brain swelling, and we had to induce a coma.
ABBIE. You induced a coma without asking me first?
DOCTOR. I'm afraid there was no other way. We should have the lab results by the end of today.

Abbie nods. The Doctor exits. Time passes. Abbie rests her head on Micah's bed.

Black.

Scene 2

In the blackout, the heartbeat sound grows longer, deeper, and slower, indicating that time has slowed. Lights up. Abbie's head still rests on the bed. ARIEL stands upstage.

ARIEL. Micah, wake up.

Micah wakes with a gasp. Abbie remains motionless.

ARIEL. It's time to go.

> *As Micah moves their hands, they realize
> they can move. Their eyes immediately find
> Abbie.*

MICAH. Hey, Abbie.
ARIEL. She's asleep. She won't hear you. Let her
    rest.

> *Micah notices Ariel.*

MICAH. Who are you?
ARIEL. You can call me Ariel.
MICAH. You're not a doctor or a nurse, are you?
      Abbie?
ARIEL. Not quite, no.
MICAH. Then what are you doing here?
ARIEL. I'm here to help.
MICAH. Like a social worker? Abbie?
ARIEL. More like a guardian angel.
MICAH. I have a guardian angel?
ARIEL. No, you don't. *(under breath)* Not anymore.
MICAH. Then what are you doing here?

> *A slow, heavy heartbeat is heard.*

ARIEL. No more questions. Time to go.
MICAH. Go where?
ARIEL. On.
MICAH. What do you mean, "on"?
ARIEL. Just on. It's time.

MICAH. You mean, like to heaven?
ARIEL. Well…
MICAH. Am I dying?
ARIEL. Yes, you are, Micah.

Micah is not ready for this. No one ever is.

MICAH. No, no, no. That can't be. I'm feeling great!
        I'm not dying. You've got the wrong person.
ARIEL. It's definitely you. Come on, let's go.
MICAH. Then how come I feel amazing? Look, I can
        move everything. I've got energy. I've got
        moves. I'm thrivin'!
ARIEL. That's what it feels like when you shed a
        human shell.
MICAH. I don't think I've ever felt better! Just just
        take someone else.
ARIEL. I can't do that.
MICAH. Like, you don't want to, or you can't?
ARIEL. I can't. It's your turn.
MICAH. What do you want? I promise I'll be good
        from here on. I'll work harder; I'll help
        others… I can go to church! I promise I'll go
        every Sunday. Every day, if you want me to.
ARIEL. I'm not here to negotiate.
MICAH. Then go away! I'm not dying today!

A very loud heartbeat interrupts them.

MICAH. What the–
ARIEL. Hear that?
MICAH. Kinda hard to miss.

ARIEL. That's your heart. It has eighty-six beats
        left
MICAH. What?
ARIEL. Then it will stop. And when it does–
MICAH. How do you know that?
ARIEL. When it does, trust me it will be a lot easier
        for everyone if you come with me
        voluntarily.
MICAH. Voluntarily? So I do have a choice?
ARIEL. Not on whether–
MICAH. I'm choosing to stay.
ARIEL. Micah–
MICAH. I can't leave.
ARIEL. Why not?
MICAH. Because of my wife.

Micah indicates Abbie.

ARIEL. Abbie.
MICAH. All my life, she's taken care of me.
ARIEL. That was very kind of her
MICAH. Since we were little kids! We're both
        orphans. Every time I got beaten up, or an
        adoption failed, or I just wanted to give up…
        she's been there for me. I owe her so much. I
        can't just leave her.
ARIEL. I can assure you, Abbie doesn't feel like you
        owe her anything.
MICAH. But she needs my help now! She just lost
        her job
ARIEL. I know.
MICAH. If I'm gone, what will happen to her?

ARIEL. She'll figure it out.
MICAH. That's all you've got? "She'll figure it out?"
          If I die, she'll be all alone.
ARIEL. She won't be alone.
MICAH. How can you know that?
ARIEL. She's got *(stops)*…friends, right?
MICAH. Yes, she does have some good friends.
ARIEL. There you go.
MICAH. But it's not the same. I want to be the one
          who is there for her. She's my wife!
ARIEL. It is not your choice when you enter this life
          or leave it. And when you cannot choose it,
          you are not responsible for the
          consequences.
MICAH. But I want to be. Please let me be.
ARIEL. There will always be things unfinished. You
          have to trust that others will finish them for
          you.

          *A moment of silence. Only the slow, heavy
          heartbeat is heard.*

ARIEL. Time is running short. We need to go.
MICAH. You're just being mean on purpose! I
          thought you were my guardian angel?
ARIEL. I'm not.
MICAH. Are you the devil? Is that what this is
          about? You're trying to make my life hell!
ARIEL. The only hell that exists is the
          powerlessness you choose.
MICAH. You sound like the devil! This is evil!

ARIEL. Stop being so childish. You were given the gift of life. It's nothing you've earned or are entitled to. Now it will be taken away. You have no right to complain.

MICAH. What about my future? All the things I didn't get to do yet? Aren't they part of the life experience?

ARIEL. Like what?

MICAH. Like... I want to grow old. With my wife. You know, sitting on a porch, drinking coffee, eating whatever I want, telling the neighbors off for being too loud or parking the wrong way... And then, my buddy and I, we've been working on this new type of bioplastic. It's so cool. It dissolves when you put it in salt water. We want to make it a business. Reduce plastic waste. Clean up the planet... do our part... And jeez, what day is it?

ARIEL. It's Friday, Micah.

MICAH. What time?

ARIEL. 6:34

MICAH. A.M. or

ARIEL. P.M. You fell into a coma earlier this morning.

MICAH. Shit! Abbie and I, we had a doctor's appointment. OBGYN. About having children. We think we're ready. For kids, I mean. We want a boy and a girl, but I'm sure we'll be happy no matter what. Our own family. I can't wait to know what that'll be like.

ARIEL. I get that.
MICAH. What about all these things? If I was given
        the gift of life, don't I have a right to the full
        experience?
ARIEL. What exactly is it that you want?
MICAH. What do you mean?
ARIEL. Growing old, why would you want that?
MICAH. So I know what it feels like!
ARIEL. Haven't you grown older since the day you
        were born?
MICAH. Yes, but–
ARIEL. Why do you want to build a business?
MICAH. So I can try new things, see what works,
        and then do it better.
ARIEL. Don't you do that every day of your life?
        Why do you want to have kids?
MICAH. So, I know what it's like to love and be
        loved eternally.
ARIEL. But you already do.

They both look at Abbie. Another heartbeat.

ARIEL. Most of what we seek has always been
        right in front of us. But it often takes the
        imminence of loss to recognize it.
MICAH. You're right. Please don't make me leave
        her.
ARIEL. It's neither your choice nor mine. Come on,
        let us go.
MICAH. But where am I going? You're not taking
        me to hell, are you?

ARIEL. You will only be in hell if you don't come
          with me now.
MICAH. But I haven't done anything bad! I haven't
          hurt anyone. I always tried my best to be
          good–
ARIEL. Yes, you did. We have to–
MICAH. Then, please, I have no place in hell. I
          belong in heaven–
ARIEL. That is not my choice to make. Time is
          running–
MICAH. Then whose choice is it? Please, wait. Are
          you quite certain that I'm dying?
ARIEL. Absolutely.
MICAH. And there's nothing that can be done
          about it? No treatment or anything?
ARIEL. Nothing at all.
MICAH. Then can you at least tell me what I'm
          facing? Will there be a test? Do I have to
          weigh my soul?
ARIEL. All I can tell you is not to worry about that,
          Micah. Please, let's just go!

The heartbeat begins to speed up again.

MICAH. How can I not worry about it?
ARIEL. Micah, we're running out of time! I need
          you to come with me!

Abbie begins to move very slowly.

MICAH. Abbie, Abbie, hey, I'm here. Can you hear
          me?

She does not react.

ARIEL. She can't hear you, Micah. Come on only
        four beats left!
MICAH. Abbie, please!
ARIEL. Three. You'll end up in hell if you stay now!
MICAH. I'm okay! I'll be fine!
ARIEL. Two. You have to go on so you can be
        reborn again!
MICAH. Just look at me, please! Abbie!
ARIEL. One. Micah, this is your last chance!

> *Abbie awakens with a gasp. The heartbeat
> monitor flatlines. Micah collapses as the
> lights go to black.
> In the dark*

ABBIE. Micah! MICAH!!! Help! Somebody! Please
        help!!!

Scene 3

> *This entire scene takes place in blackout.
> The door bursts open, followed by the
> sound of the Nurse's footsteps entering the
> room.*

NURSE. Code blue! Doctor to 204!

> *The Doctor rushes in, pushing a crash cart.*

ABBIE. Micah, don't leave me!
NURSE. BP's dropping, no pulse!
DOCTOR. Starting compressions! Charge to 200
     joules.
NURSE. Charging... Clear!

The sound of a defibrillator.

DOCTOR. Still no rhythm. Charge to 300.
ABBIE. Micah!
DOCTOR. Oxygen stats critical.
NURSE. Charging... Clear!

The sound of a second defibrillator attempt.

DOCTOR. Nothing. One more time. Charge to 360.
NURSE. Charging... Clear!
ABBIE. Come back to me! Please!

The sound of a third defibrillator attempt.
Finally, the heartbeat monitor resumes.

NURSE. We've got a rhythm!
DOCTOR. He's back.
ABBIE. Micah...

Scene 4

Lights up. Micah lies in bed, motionless. The
steady heartbeat can be heard. Abbie

stands on one side of the bed; Ariel stands on the other.

ARIEL. *(to Micah)* I'm so sorry, Micah. You could have chosen your next life, but you chose hell instead.

The Doctor enters, addressing Abbie.

DOCTOR. The worst has been confirmed. It's bacterial meningitis. Micah will never wake up again.

Abbie breaks into tears.

ARIEL. *(to Micah)* It wasn't my place to answer your questions. You see, I'm not *your* guardian angel *(turns to Abbie)* but *hers.*

Ariel approaches Abbie and gently places a hand on her shoulder.

DOCTOR. There is no hope for recovery. Micah left you in charge. Sooner or later, you will have to make a very hard decision.

Abbie looks up.

ABBIE. I don't understand. You're going to make me kill the love of my life?

End of play.

THE HELPER'S HAND

by Niki J. Borger

Overview
A 10-minute comedy
for 3 actors of any gender and 1 female VO

Synopsis
When guardian angel Ariel attempts to give up
their wings, their colleagues help them get back on
track.

Characters
ARIEL   – any age
RIB   – any age
CRICKET   – any age
ABBIE   – female, 20s to 30s, voice-over

Setting
A guardian angel office in heaven. A punch clock
sits next to the door, along with desks, case files,
and success snapshots.
Downstage center is an invisible gateway to Earth,
functioning as a viewing portal through which
characters can glimpse human life below and, when
entering it, ascend into human form.

Scene 1

Lights up on ARIEL, sitting at the Earth Gateway, watching ABBIE below.

ABBIE. *(v.o.)* Please let him come back to me. Please, please, please...

CRICKET enters, punches in, yawns, and approaches their desk.

CRICKET. Didn't hear the word God in there.
ARIEL. She's not religious.
CRICKET. In times like this, people tend to try anyway. Just in case there's something to it after all.
ARIEL. And here we are, knowing it's not that simple...

Ariel pulls away from the Earth Gateway. Cricket approaches it and flips through their cases while watching Ariel out of the corner of their eye.

CRICKET. Shouldn't you be down there with her?
ARIEL. I should.
CRICKET. I'm confused.
ARIEL. That makes two of us.
CRICKET. I'm even more confused.

Ariel takes a moment before admitting

ARIEL. I don't think I can do this job anymore.
CRICKET. Guarding?
ARIEL. Angeling.

> *Cricket flips the Earth Gateway back to
> Abbie, then waits for Ariel to elaborate
> while pouring a hot drink from a large
> amphora into two mugs.*

ARIEL. They think we're all good, and happy, and
      filled with love. That we have all the answers
CRICKET. We do
ARIEL. Then why do we fail sometimes? Why
      couldn't I protect her? Why couldn't I find
      the right words? Why couldn't I just make
      him... you know... I feel like such a cheat!
CRICKET. Did you rest at all?

> *Cricket places a warm mug into Ariel's
> hands, but Ariel does not drink.*

ARIEL. I've decided to hand in my wings.
CRICKET. Nonsense.
ARIEL. I mean it.
CRICKET. And leave us?
ARIEL. Yeah.
CRICKET. To do what?
ARIEL. I don't know
CRICKET. Where?
ARIEL. I don't know
CRICKET. Who will do your work?
ARIEL. I don't know, Cricket, I don't know!

CRICKET. We're already short-staffed, and Black
        Monday is around the corner.

Ariel doesn't respond.

CRICKET. You'd just leave us hanging. I thought we
        were friends.
ARIEL. We are
CRICKET. *(digresses into a rare, emotional
        tantrum)* Plus, the whole thing could set a
        precedent. Angels could start handing in
        their wings left and right. Humans would go
        unprotected. The remaining guardians
        would be overwhelmed. It'd be mayhem in
        heaven! *(to Ariel)* And that would be on you!

*Cricket shudders and takes a sip from their
mug, then exhales, releasing their tension.
Ariel takes a sip as well and immediately
relaxes. Cricket sits beside Ariel.*

CRICKET. Did you try your best?
ARIEL. Of course I did.
CRICKET. How did you do it?
ARIEL. I was kind and supportive. He was dead
        scared, of course–

Cricket laughs at the unintended joke.

ARIEL. He was really scared of dying–

*RIB enters, punches in, and joins the
conversation.*

RIB. Mornin'
CRICKET. Good morning, Rib
ARIEL. So I tried to comfort him and take away his
		fears.

		*Rib goes to get a drink, but the amphora is
		empty.*

CRICKET. That was the mistake.
ARIEL. Why?
RIB. Humans rarely grow from love. They grow
		from fear. You should have made him more
		afraid of the consequences.

		*Rib takes an empty cup, hands it to Cricket,
		takes Cricket's full cup instead, and takes a
		sip.*

RIB. We're out of love, boss.
ARIEL. That sounds horrible.
CRICKET. Maybe. But it works.

		Cricket rises and approaches the amphora.

RIB. Right you are. What's the trouble?
CRICKET. Ariel went all nice on a human in an
		attempt to convince him to die, and that
		didn't work.
RIB. Ah.

CRICKET. Now his wife is all upset because she has
        to kill him.

Cricket magics the amphora, refilling it.

RIB. Classic. Can't leave him, so she's murdering
        him instead.
ARIEL. That's not
CRICKET. Wives don't always have a choice
ARIEL. It's not
RIB. And husbands often deserve it
ARIEL. It's not
RIB. Love a good revenge story
CRICKET. When it's grounded in justice
RIB. So satisfying

Cricket fills a mug from the amphora.

ARIEL. They're not like that. She loves him, he
        loves her. But he's in a coma. He'll never
        wake up, and now she has to be the one to
        turn off the machines.
RIB. Oh... that's bad.
CRICKET. Really bad.
RIB. And you messed that one up?
ARIEL. I think I did.
CRICKET. *(dryly)* Have some warm love.

*Cricket places the fresh mug into Ariel's
hand, takes the old one, and drinks.*

ABBIE. *(v.o.)* Please, God

CRICKET. There it is
ABBIE. *(v.o.)* If you're out there, help me. Let him
        go the natural way. And if you can't, let me
        go instead. Just don't make me do this…
CRICKET. All right, time for you to get down there.

*Cricket begins pushing Ariel toward the
Earth Gateway.*

ARIEL. I can't. I really can't. I'm going to hand in my
        wings instead.
RIB. What?
ARIEL. It's better for everyone. I'm no good as an
        angel, so I'd rather do what's best and
        resign.
RIB. Best for everyone or best for yourself?
ARIEL. Sorry?
RIB. Sounds like you're bailing to me.
ARIEL. I want what's best for her.
CRICKET. Get down there now!
ARIEL. I can't. I don't have it in me.
RIB. Then it's best for yourself to quit.
ARIEL. You're being a bit mean right now.
RIB. Am I?
CRICKET. You are, but that's not the point.
RIB. Then what is the point?
CRICKET. This isn't rocket science! *(to Ariel)* You
        look at her.

Cricket points toward the Earth Gateway.

CRICKET. What do you see?

ARIEL. Abbie, sitting next to Micah's bed, crying.
CRICKET. *A human in need of comfort.*
ARIEL. Right.
CRICKET. So what should you give her?
ARIEL. Comfort.
CRICKET. Right. *(beat)* Now think of a man
        choosing between his own death and his
        wife's ongoing suffering. What do they
        need?
RIB. And we're talking about a real man here, not a
        whiny little flake
ARIEL. That's an awful choice to make. They need
        comfort, too.
CRICKET. Wrong!
RIB. They need some serious ass-whooping.
CRICKET. Exactly.
RIB. Put them in their place
CRICKET. Remind them of their priorities
RIB. And the chance to be *a hero*
CRICKET. Right. They have no power but that one
        choice.
RIB. Make them feel it.
CRICKET. They will either die a hero or betray
        everything they swore to protect.
RIB. Whoo, intense.
ARIEL. Okay... so I should have told Micah what
        would be happening.
CRICKET. Probably.
RIB. Or just scared him enough
CRICKET. That works too. *(beat)* Now, think of a
        human who puts all their effort into denying
        what's real.

ARIEL. Like Abbie right now? She thinks there's
        still hope for Micah to wake up.
CRICKET. Is there?
ARIEL. No.
CRICKET. Then yes, she is in denial about that.
RIB. And something else.
ARIEL. What's that?
RIB. Think hard.
CRICKET. Something she just said.
ARIEL. The belief that it's better for her life to end
        than to carry the responsibility of ending
        his... the fear that... that responsibility will
        bury her anyway.
CRICKET. Huge denial.
RIB. Massive.
ARIEL. It feels true to her.
RIB. And that's where you come in.
CRICKET. What does she need?
ARIEL. Not ass-whooping, I'm sure.
CRICKET. No.
RIB. But similar.
CRICKET. She needs someone to set her straight.
RIB. Mind-whooping, you could say
CRICKET. Brutal honesty
ARIEL. About what?
RIB. Come on, angel. You know that one.

        *Ariel takes a deep breath and closes their
        eyes for a moment.*

ARIEL. That she still has so much life ahead of her.
        That she's actually helping him. That she will

recover, and that the best parts have yet to
come.
CRICKET. Precisely.

*Ariel relaxes slightly and takes another sip
from their mug.*

RIB. Now, last one.

Cricket looks confused.

RIB. Think of an angel with a big heart and a
beautiful smile, who is burned out from
caring for humans. What does she need?

Ariel smiles faintly.

ARIEL. A hug?

*Ariel moves in for a hug, but Rib holds them
at arm's length.*

RIB. No. Boundaries. You don't carry their burdens.
ARIEL. Right.
CRICKET. And it's not your job to sacrifice
yourself. Remember, the helper's hand can
only give what it has in abundance.

Ariel nods.
Rib then pulls Ariel into a hug.

RIB. Come here. Better?

ARIEL. Much better.
CRICKET. Good. You have a job to do.

Ariel nods and smiles.

RIB. Excited?
ARIEL. Yes. Not about the job, but... I've been with
        her, her entire life... and this will be the first
        time she will see me.

They share a smile. Lights fade.

End of play.

CRASH / KILL

by Niki J. Borger

Overview
A 10-minute drama
for 3 actors and 1 VO of any gender

Synopsis
When losing control of their car on a rainy bridge,
Riley must choose between hitting and killing
another person or sacrificing themselves.

Characters
RILEY   – 30s to 50s
RIB   – any age
CASEY   – 16 to 22
NEWS ANCHOR   – voice-over

Setting
1989. A narrow, aging bridge just outside Seattle.
Heavy rain. Split stage. On one side, Riley sits
behind the steering wheel of a vintage Camaro. On
the other side, Casey is also behind a steering
wheel.

Notes
All characters may be any gender. Riley's driving
movements should mirror Casey's with a slight
delay. All driving action should be supported by
appropriate sound effects, including windshield

wipers, turn signals, horns, brakes, and other vehicle sounds.

Scene 1

Upon rise, the stage is split exactly in the middle. Both RILEY and CASEY are driving their vehicles at speed through heavy rain. Riley's movements mirror Casey's with a slight delay. Both are laser-focused, listening to the radio.

NEWS ANCHOR. ...voters have elected African-American council member Norm Rice as the first Black mayor of Seattle. In his acceptance speech, Rice emphasized the importance of taking a stand for the needy and uniting the people of this great city. And now the weather for Friday, November 8, 1989: heavy rains will continue throughout the weekend as

Simultaneously, Riley and Casey turn off their radios and continue driving. The lights around them dim first around Casey, then around Riley as they turn onto smaller and smaller country roads. The rain intensifies, and the windshield wipers move faster. Casey's tire hits a pothole, and they hit the brakes.

CASEY. Jesus!

A second later, Riley hits the brakes as well, honking at the car ahead.

RILEY. Move it, asshole!

Riley continues honking at Casey. Slowly, Casey begins driving again, followed by Riley. A traffic light appears. Casey makes it through just before it turns red, but Riley is stopped at the red.

RILEY. Who the fuck needs a traffic light in the middle of nowhere?

Riley turns the radio back on and begins tapping the steering wheel aggressively to the beat. Casey continues driving, picking up speed. The car enters the bridge. Riley gets a green light and begins driving again. Casey speeds up further and, as something suddenly crosses in front of the car

CASEY. Shit!

They hit the brakes, and the car begins to aquaplane. It strikes the sides of the bridge, left, then right, spinning the vehicle, before the rear end hits the left side again, and the car comes to a stop.

Riley continues driving, tapping along to the beat of the song and singing. Casey, dizzy and disoriented, tries to orient themselves inside the car. They unbuckle their seat belt, find the door handle, and pull; it's stuck. After throwing themselves against the door several times, it finally opens.

Riley continues driving, faster and faster, singing along.

Casey stumbles out of the car. The headlights of Casey's car begin to shine directly into Riley's face. They both look up simultaneously.

RILEY and CASEY. NO!

Scene 2

Time slows to an almost complete halt. The music stops; all sound fades. Darkness. Then a soft light slowly rises on Riley alone, still wide-eyed, mouth open from the scream. They begin to relax, look around, but fail to notice RIB, who stands just behind them.

RILEY. What is happening?
RIB. Time for your reckoning.

*Rib steps into view. Riley stumbles
backward.*

RILEY. Jeez motherfucker!
RIB. Don't wet yourself.
RILEY. Who are you?
RIB. The question is, who are you?
RILEY. Why is everything frozen?
RIB. You're about to crash.
RILEY. Fuck off
RIB. You can either hit that car and kill the driver,
        or swerve and sacrifice yourself.
RILEY. What?
RIB. Which one will it be, Riley?
RILEY. How do you know my name?
RIB. Crash or kill?
RILEY. "Kill" is a bit harsh. It would be an accident.
RIB. You were speeding.
RILEY. They were speeding, too!
RIB. Deflection. Really?
RILEY. They crashed first! They're in the way!
RIB. So you weren't tailgating?
RILEY. I'm in a hurry, all right? I need to get to my
        sister.
RIB. Not tonight.
RILEY. She's in the hospital.
RIB. You won't see her tonight.
RILEY. Fuck this. I don't believe you. This is all in my
        head.
RIB. Don't believe me, believe him.

Rib guides Riley's gaze forward. In the distance, Casey stands, frozen in place.

Scene 3

Lights up on Casey. They see the approaching car and instantly understand what it means.

CASEY. They say you'll see your life flash before your eyes right before you die. And here it is. My first memory is my mother pushing me in a pram at night to ease my croup. The time I fell off the swings in kindergarten and bit a hole through my tongue. Learning to ride a bicycle with my grandpa. Getting my first dog, Emma, a little Chihuahua, for my sixth birthday. The first time I hit a home run in baseball. That exchange student I really liked in middle school. Seeing the pride in my dad's eyes when I got accepted into college to become a doctor, like him. My mother's tears when the police told her he had died in a car crash. It's all there. Twenty-one years of living.

Lights dim on Casey.

Scene 4

RILEY. Okay, okay... it sounds like it's already decided, doesn't it? He sees his life flashing; he'll die. There's nothing I can do about it.

RIB. Coward

RILEY. But I don't want to die either!

RIB. So you'll kill someone else?

RILEY. It's not killing if it's an accident. I'm not pointing a gun at his head. I didn't choose for him to end up like this, in my way.

RIB. That tracks.

RILEY. I'm just saying we were both speeding. That makes him no better than me. Why should I die for him?

RIB. Not an ounce of self-responsibility...

RILEY. This is on him! Not on me. Why should I be the one to make the sacrifice?

RIB. Fine. Go kill someone else, then. But do me a favor

Rib grabs Riley and forces them to look forward.

RIB. At least look into his face when you do it. Look into his eyes. See the soul whose life you're ending.

RILEY. He's just a kid.

RIB. Exactly.

Riley pulls free from Rib's grip.

RILEY. Fuck! I don't want to die, man. I can't die.
RIB. Everyone dies. Isn't that what you always say?
RILEY. Yeah, but
RIB. When you're selling insurance?
RILEY. That's my job
RIB. To people who can't afford it?
RILEY. It's how the business works.
RIB. Sure works well for you, leech.
RILEY. Come on, man, nobody's perfect.
RIB. You certainly aren't.

Scene 5

Lights up on Casey.

CASEY. It's my mother I'm rushing to see. How stupid driving that fast in all this rain. I should've been more careful. I could slap myself for it... But thinking of her, lying alone in that hospital bed, not knowing what got her there in the first place or what will happen next, what will she do without me? What will she do when she finds out her only child died the same way her husband did? How will she find the strength to go on when she realizes she's all alone?

Lights dim again

Scene 6

RILEY. It's my nephew. This is my nephew, Casey.
　　　Fuck... fuck, fuck, fuck!
RIB. Catching on, eh?
RILEY. This is fucked up! Capital F, fucked up!
RIB. F-bombs won't help.
RILEY. Fuck! You can't be serious. I can't kill my
　　　nephew, that's not a choice! What kind of
　　　masochistic asshole are you? There has to
　　　be another way!
RIB. You tell me. You're on a bridge covered in
　　　water. You either go straight or you swerve,
　　　break through the barrier, and hit the river
　　　below. Unless you can grow wings?

*Riley moves in front of the car and pushes,
attempting to stop it.*

RILEY. Let's stop the car. Right now. You and me.
　　　Come on, give me a hand here.
RIB. This is all in your head, man.
RILEY. I can't be the reason for my nephew's
　　　death!
RIB. Then don't.
RILEY. But I really don't want to die!
RIB. If you don't choose soon, there will be no help
　　　for either one of you.
RILEY. What about my sister? What will happen to
　　　her if I die?
RIB. What will happen if she finds out you killed
　　　her son?

RILEY. She wouldn't have to know, would she?
RIB. Still wiggling your way out. For once in your
         life, don't run!
RILEY. This is an impossible choice!
RIB. Choose now, or it'll be too late!
RILEY. I can't!
RIB. If the roles were flipped, what do you think he
         would do?
RILEY. I don't know…

*The lights rise again on Casey. Slowly, the
ambient sounds return and build in
intensity.*

CASEY. God, Yahweh, Allah, I don't really believe in
         any of you, but… whatever it is that's out
         there
RILEY. As if that will help
RIB. Clock's ticking, Riley
CASEY. Please protect my mom. Help her become
         healthy again
RILEY. Prayer won't save anyone!
RIB. You can save him!
CASEY. She'll be heartbroken. Help her heal, and
         one day, maybe find hope again
RILEY. Stop showing me this
RIB. You're the one seeing it
RILEY. I don't want to
CASEY. If this is really my time, it would be nice if
         you could make it quick and painless
RILEY. Oh, fuck off
RIB. You can stop it, Riley

CASEY. And if there is a heaven, please let me in.
RILEY. Get away from me
RIB. Man up, Riley
CASEY. I always tried to do the right thing
RILEY. Fuck, fuck, FUCK!
RIB. Last chance, Riley

> *Riley rushes back behind the steering wheel.*

CASEY. And if I can't go to heaven, please send someone else to look over my mom

> *Riley screams. At the last moment, Riley yanks the steering wheel away from Casey. Sound returns fully as Riley's car breaks through the barrier, metal-tearing, glass-shattering, but the rear of the car still strikes Casey. Everything goes dark. Silence.*

Scene 7

> *A car radio is turned on.*

NEWS ANCHOR. *(o.s.)* The Mayfly Bridge remains closed this morning following a fatal two-car accident late last night. Authorities say both vehicles appear to have lost control due to wet conditions, with early police reports indicating aquaplaning before the second car struck the first. Both drivers were pronounced dead at the scene.

The radio is switched off.

RIB. *(o.s.).* This wasn't about changing the outcome, Riley. It was about who you'd be when it came down to it. You tried to save the kid. That counts. Your slate is clean. You're ready for your next life.

End of play.

Teddy Bears and Scented Candles

by Niki J. Borger

Overview
A 15-minute comedy
For 2 actors (1 female, 1 any gender) and 3 VO (1 male, 2 any gender)

Synopsis
In the afterlife, a soul desperate to remain with her best friend will try anything to keep them from reincarnating back to Earth.

Characters
JEN   –late teens to late 20s, female, person of color
CASEY   –late teens to late 20s
VOICE   –any age, heavenly presence, voice-over
MIDWIFE   –30s to 60s, voice-over
DAD   – 20s to 50s, male, voice-over

Setting
A luminous, undefined space, heaven, or a waiting room just before rebirth. The environment is simple and ethereal, with pale or white tones.

Five distinct "stations" are arranged throughout the space, each representing a facet of life design:
• Challenges (e.g., poverty, chronic illness)
• Crossroads (e.g., marriage, abortion)
• Potentials (e.g., hidden talent, life-changing encounter)
• Inevitables (e.g., accident, pandemic)
• Blessings (e.g., intuition, lifelong friend)

These stations may be represented abstractly (pedestals, symbols, objects, pools of light) or as minimal markers, depending on the tone and production budget.

Downstage center is an invisible Gateway to Earth, serving as a viewing portal through which characters can glimpse earthly life below and, eventually, enter their incarnation.

Upstage or tucked subtly in a corner is a large, inconspicuous dark bag.

Notes
The date on the incarnations clipboard should be updated to match the performance date.

Scene 1

Lights up. JEN, clipboard in hand, watches intently through the Earth Gateway. Downstage, CASEY carefully spreads a square of soft white fabric, preparing to pack their karmic bundle, the blueprint of their next life.

JEN. She's dying her hair.
CASEY. So what?
JEN. It means she already has gray hair at thirty-three. You don't want that, do you?
CASEY. It's not that big of a deal.
JEN. They're using scented candles.
CASEY. I like scented candles.
JEN. They're disgusting! They're always fake, the smell gets everywhere, and you can never get rid of it again!

Jen mimics throwing up.

CASEY. You're so dramatic.

Jen mimics Casey. Satisfied with their packing area, Casey turns toward the different types of life experiences.

CASEY. Time to pack. Let's see...

Casey makes their way toward the first station: Challenges.

VOICE. *(o.s.)* Choose three life challenges that support your soul's growth and expansion.

Casey begins looking through the challenges, picking them up and tossing them aside casually.

JEN *(very dramatically).* He just prayed! The guy just prayed to God!

CASEY. And?

JEN. Jeez, Casey! The beliefs you'd grow up with! The rules! All the condemnation, the talk about hell and death, all the guilt-tripping! Your life is going to be awful!

Casey turns toward Jen.

CASEY. Okay, stop it, Jen. They're good people. They'll be great parents. I've made my choice.

JEN. Well, what about me?

CASEY. What about you?

JEN. It says here that they'll only have one child.

Jen indicates the clipboard in her hand. It is labeled: "Incarnations 2026-05-01, 9:20–9:21 p.m."

CASEY. Just pick one of their friends.

Jen skims the pages. Casey continues selecting life challenges.

JEN. But none of their friends wants any more kids.

CASEY. Someone on their street.
JEN. No, no one.
CASEY. Then the neighborhood.
JEN. The neighborhood? That's too far.
CASEY. What do you mean?
JEN. Neighborhoods are big.
CASEY. Theirs isn't.
JEN. We may never meet.
CASEY. You'll just have to make an effort!

Casey has picked three life challenges and places them in their bundle.

JEN. How can I make an effort if I won't even remember?
CASEY. You'll figure it out.
JEN. Casey!

Jen stops Casey.

JEN. I feel like you're not taking this seriously. This is a big deal for both of us. The decision you make now will impact your entire next life.
CASEY. I know. That's why I picked them. Laura and Henry Stegent. And I'll be their daughter, Alice. It's going to be great!
JEN. But I thought we said we'd incarnate together so we can be friends again in that life.
CASEY. Yes! That's why I brought the list so you can pick someone you like.

*Casey indicates the clipboard, then
something "below" catches their attention.*

CASEY. You may want to hurry up, though. It looks
        like Henry's about to make his move.
JEN. What?
CASEY. He's about to, you know, knock boots, get
        busy
JEN. What?
CASEY. They're about to make a baby! And I don't
        want to miss this opportunity and stay stuck
        here for another month.

*Jen glances at the list, then throws it away.
She approaches the large, dark bag at the
back and begins pulling it downstage. Casey
picks up the clipboard.*

CASEY. How about them? Gerald and Emily
        Watson.
JEN. Her family has the breast cancer gene.
CASEY. So?
JEN. I don't want to die young again. I want to grow
        old.
CASEY. Okay. Here, Miranda and Steve Michaels.
        They seem healthy. And very well settled.
JEN. Yeah, but look at their karmic luggage:
        betrayal, greed, exploitation. Yikes. Plus, I
        don't want to be born white.
CASEY. Why not?
JEN. I just like being a minority better. Gives me
        more rights to complain.

CASEY. Whatever… okay, here Simone and Lloyd Washington. Mixed race. Middle class. Healthy genetics. Plus, they live only a couple of streets away from my parents.

JEN. But they're deeply wounded, look at that. Rejection for her and neglect for him. Ugh, what a mix. First, I won't like anything about myself, and then I won't even have the courage to talk about it.

CASEY. Honestly, Jen, you're too picky!

JEN. I'm not. I just know what I want!

CASEY. And what's that?

JEN. Stay here, where everything is perfect, and have a good time with you.

They look at each other for a moment. Then Casey hands the list back to Jen, who drops the bag.

CASEY. But I want to go. I feel like I'm ready.

Casey proceeds to the second station: Crossroads.

VOICE. *(o.s.)* Choose the crossroads in your next life.

JEN. Are you, though?

CASEY. What do you mean?

JEN. Are you ready? I'm just saying… it hasn't been that long since you passed. Since we both passed.

CASEY. So what?

JEN. Dying young is entirely underestimated. It creates a subconscious fear that everything is dangerous. And you'll carry that with you as soon as you're back in a human body.

CASEY. Well, I have to deal with it sooner or later.

JEN. Unless you stay here…

Casey rolls their eyes.

JEN. If you don't deal with it properly, you might just manifest it again!

CASEY. What are you talking about?

JEN. It's your karmic luggage. It's part of your vibration, your subconscious. If you're not careful, it may become so strong that you manifest it again, and then you die, and once more, you're leaving your parents heartbroken. Do you really want to do that to… *(checks the list)* poor Laura and Henry?

Casey adds their crossroads to their bundle when, again, something "below" catches their attention.

CASEY. Oh, look, he's giving her a plushie.

JEN. Fantastic. Teddy bears. Yay…

CASEY. Yup. Teddy bears and scented candles. Can't wait.

Jen mimics throwing up again. Casey proceeds to the third station: Potentials.

VOICE. *(o.s.)* Choose what may happen in your
          next life.
CASEY. You know it's your choice what karmic
          luggage you take, right? *(indicating Jen's
          bag)* You could just leave that and pack
          something new.
JEN. And forget everything that's evil and bad and
          dangerous down there? No way!
CASEY. You're such an old soul. Look, if I die young
          again, then it'll be because it's the best path
          for my soul and everyone involved, not
          because of some manifested fear. No fear
          can ever be stronger than the soul's choice
          of when to die and when to live again.
JEN. You can't know that for sure.
CASEY. I am sure.
JEN. But better safe than sorry. Let's just stay here,
          give yourself some time to process, to heal
          those old wounds before you incarnate back
          on Earth.
CASEY. Jen, we're not processing anything here.
          We just are. And I don't want to just be, I
          want to do things, experience things, feel
          things again. I'm ready.
JEN. But I'm not.
CASEY. You're not ready to be human again?
JEN. I'm not ready to go back down there. I don't
          want to.
CASEY. You don't like the freedom of being alive?

          *Casey adds their potentials to their karmic
          bundle. Jen approaches the Challenges*

station.

JEN. How can you call it freedom when there are
        so many things I don't get to do? Or be?
CASEY. Like what?
JEN. Like becoming the president, for example.
CASEY. You can become the president if you like.
JEN. Yeah, sure. And *misogyny (she indicates the
        equivalent option from the station)* isn't
        standing in my way at all.
CASEY. Come on, Jen–
JEN. No woman has ever been elected president in
        this country!
CASEY. Maybe you'll be the first.
JEN. Right.
CASEY. What else?
JEN. Maybe I want to be a CEO.
CASEY. You can be a CEO. You just have to work
        your way up
JEN. Sure, that's how it works. Once *systemic
        racism* and *nepotism* are gone.

        *She again indicates the equivalents in the
        Challenges station.*

CASEY. You could incarnate as a rich white boy.

        Jen throws Casey a glance that says it all.

CASEY. I feel like this has nothing to do with job
        options.
JEN. You're right... look...

Casey suddenly notices something below.

CASEY. Goodness! They're already at it!
JEN. What?

Jen joins Casey at the Gateway, and they watch for a moment.

CASEY. Is that–
JEN. Wow.
CASEY. I need to go!

Casey rushes to the fourth station: Inevitables.

VOICE. *(o.s.)* Choose what will happen in your next life, no matter what.
JEN. Wait, Casey, one second, please.
CASEY. Please, Jen, just pick someone and let's go.
JEN. Do you love me?
CASEY. Of course I do. And I don't want you to be left behind. Come on!
JEN. But just like casual love, or more like real–
CASEY. All love is real, Jen.

Casey adds their inevitables to their bundle.

JEN. That's not... Casey... please, just hold off and look at me for a second.

Jen stops Casey.

JEN. In the next life, I want us to be more than
          just… friends.
CASEY. Like…
JEN. I love you, Casey. And I want to spend my next
          life with you.
CASEY. Jen… you know we can't plan on that.
          Neither of us will remember that this ever
          happened.
JEN. Right.
CASEY. We just have to hope for the best.
JEN. Or stay here. Please.

          Casey makes their way to the fifth station:
          Blessings.

VOICE. *(o.s.)* Choose as many blessings as your
          heart desires.
CASEY. Jen, I love you, you know that. But I don't
          want to stay here. I want to live again.
JEN. By yourself.
CASEY. By myself, or with you, it doesn't matter. I
          just like being alive.
JEN. It doesn't matter?
CASEY. That's not what I meant.
JEN. That is what you said.
CASEY. Yes, but I meant that my life will be great
          no matter what.
JEN. So that is what you meant. Wow!
CASEY. Don't be upset.
JEN. Upset? I'm not upset! I'm heartbroken, Casey!
CASEY. Really, it's not that big of a deal. You know
          how life works

JEN. I sure do

CASEY. I just mean we'll be fine no matter what.

JEN. But I don't

CASEY. If it's not with one another, then it's with
          someone else.

JEN. I don't want anyone else!

CASEY. That's not really our place to–

Again, Casey notices something below.

CASEY. Crap, I really need to go!

*Casey grabs a handful of blessings and
throws them into the bundle, then ties it.*

JEN. I killed myself for you, Casey!

CASEY. Huh?

JEN. After your accident, the car crash on the
          bridge, I killed myself so we could be
          together in heaven.

CASEY. I thought you died from–

JEN. I lied! I didn't want to be without you, so I
          killed myself.

CASEY. Jen...

JEN. And I don't want to be without you now, so
          I'm begging you, please don't leave me.

CASEY. Jen, I can't promise that we will meet or
          that I'll remember. But know this: I love you,
          and I will always love you in this lifetime and
          every one that follows. Nothing will ever
          change that. And I can't wait to get to know

you, once again, in this new life I'm about to start.

Casey takes the bundle and approaches the Earth Gateway, ready to jump. The lights around them grow very bright.

CASEY. See you soon!
JEN. Casey, please don't go! Please!

A flash of light, then darkness.

Scene 2

Lights back up. Casey is gone. Jen starts throwing a tantrum, growing more frantic by the second.

JEN. *(mimicking Casey)* It's all gonna be fine, Jen. Love will make it happen, Jen.

She picks up the list.

JEN. Love isn't making this happen, I am! Fuck this shit!

She closes her eyes and takes several deep breaths. The clock is ticking, and she knows it. She slams her finger down onto the paper.

JEN. Racial trauma and sarcasm. Great. Abigail and Joseph Whitney. And… Therese? What kind of a girl's name is that? Fuck!

She throws the clipboard aside and drags her karmic luggage bag toward the Earth Gateway.

JEN. Ugh… why is this thing so heavy?!

She reaches the very edge of the Earth Gateway.

JEN. Eww… it's going to be cold, and wet, and gross…

She steels herself, preparing to jump.

JEN. I hate being born…

The lights fade without a flash. In the darkness:

JEN. I changed my mind! I don't want to do this… No! Ouch! Leave me… no, no, no, this is too tight! No, don't do this to me… please… stop… I don't want to–

Her voice transforms into a baby's cries.

MIDWIFE. *(o.s.)* Congratulations. You have a healthy little baby girl!

DAD. *(o.s.)* You sure that's ours? She looks kind of grumpy. *(beat)* I'm joking!

End of play.

QUARTERLIFE CHECK-UP

by Niki J. Borger

Overview
A 15-minute drama
for 2 actors and 1 VO of any gender

Synopsis
When suffering a critical heart attack, Sai is given
one last chance to open their heart.

Characters
SAI   – 20s to 40s
CRICKET   – any age
BOBBY   – 20s to 40s, voice-over

Setting
2020. A small apartment in New Jersey.

Scene 1

*Lights up on a meticulously clean,
organized, minimalist apartment. After
unlocking the front door, SAI enters
wearing rubber gloves and a face mask,
carrying a week's worth of mail.*

*Sai slips off their shoes, nudges them neatly
into place, sets down the mail, removes the*

gloves, throws them in the garbage, and finally takes off the mask. For good measure, Sai sprays their hands, their mail, and then their face with disinfectant spray, coughing slightly in response.

Sai feels a brief pain in the chest. It passes.

Sai's phone rings. Sai looks at it, hesitates for a moment, then sets it down and turns their attention to the mail instead. Most of it goes into the trash; the rest is immediately sorted and placed in its proper location.

When finished, Sai looks at the phone again, then plays the voicemail they received. Meanwhile, Sai selects a ready-to-eat salad from the fridge, settles onto the couch, and chooses a show to watch.

BOBBY. *(v.o.)* Bonjour, ma chérie! Comment ça va? My French is getting better, isn't it? Now I've had time to study… I was going to ask if you wanted to hang out tonight… or tomorrow. Really, any time works. I just want to see you, it's been forever. I miss you, Sai. A lot, actually. This whole stay-at-home thing is hard enough, but I really don't want to keep doing it without you. And I know you're probably listening to this message right now, and you're worried about leaving your place and getting sick and stuff, so I can come to yours. Don't worry, I haven't been anywhere else, and I'm perfectly healthy. And I can bring actual food, not another grocery store salad, so… I'm going to call you again in a few. Please make up your mind, and please say yes. I miss you, Sai.

Sai considers this for a moment. Sai sets the salad aside, swipes through a few photos on their phone, then rubs their chest, which feels unusually cold, before pulling a blanket over their legs.

The phone rings again. Sai doesn't answer. It keeps ringing. Sai still doesn't answer. It continues ringing.

Eventually, Sai grabs the phone and puts it as far away as possible, but it continues ringing. Sai places it under a pillow, then inside their bag, but the ringing persists. Finally, Sai puts the phone inside their microwave in the kitchenette and closes the door. The ringing stops.

Sai returns to the couch and their salad. As they sit, Sai is struck by a sudden, sharp pain in their chest, then in their left arm. Dizziness overtakes them as Sai slides down onto the couch, struggling to breathe. Their breath grows shallow. Everything begins to blur.

At the same time, the lights around Sai dim until they are isolated in a single pool of light, surrounded by darkness.

CRICKET appears out of nowhere.

CRICKET. Welcome, Sai. This is your quarter-life check-up. My name is Cricket, and I'll be taking care of you today.

SAI. A doctor. I need a doctor.

CRICKET. Not just yet. We have a few minutes before any severe damage occurs, and we shall make good use of them, shan't we?

Sai begins looking for their phone.

SAI. My phone… Call an ambulance…

Cricket pulls out a clipboard and begins flipping through it.

CRICKET. You've taken very good care of your body. Full marks on that. And you're being as responsible with your life as anyone can be. But your heart… your heart is not doing well at all.

SAI. No kiddin'…

CRICKET. And that is largely due to you lying to yourself about how you truly feel. So on a

scale from one to ten, how happy are you
with your life?

SAI. I need an ambulance.

CRICKET. By general regulations, I am not
supposed to directly interfere in earthly
matters. Please answer the question.

SAI. Seven.

*Each time a number is spoken, Cricket
writes it down in her notes on the clipboard.*

CRICKET. Seven. On a scale from one to ten, how
much joy do you experience each day?

SAI. Five.

CRICKET. Five. On a scale from one to ten, how
much love is in your life?

SAI. If I answer, will you call an ambulance for me?

CRICKET. If you answer, I might consider it.

Sai tries to scream for help, but struggles.

SAI. Help... help...

CRICKET. Sai. I know you've always dreaded this,
having a medical emergency you can't solve
on your own, and no one to help you. It's
every hyper-independent person's
nightmare.

SAI. Please help me.

CRICKET. Honesty is your best medicine right
now.

SAI. Please help me.

CRICKET. Please be honest. On a scale from one to
        ten, how much love is in your life?
SAI. Two.
CRICKET. Two. Why two?
SAI. One for myself. One for that stray that follows
        me.
CRICKET. Are you referring to

Cricket checks her notes.

CRICKET. Mister Robert Chesney, nicknamed
        Bobby.
SAI. No. A cat.
CRICKET. How come Mister Robert Chesney is not
        included in your answer?
SAI. He doesn't love me. He just loves the way I
        make him feel.
CRICKET. And how is that?
SAI. Special. *(beat)* And when that stops, he'll leave.
        People always do. They only stay as long as
        you're useful to them.

The pain in Sai's chest intensifies.

CRICKET. I doubt Mister Robert Chesney would
        confirm this viewpoint.
SAI. He's unaware.
CRICKET. Or it is simply your perception. *(reads
        from Sai's past)* It is astonishing how one
        small memory from childhood can recreate
        so much pain in adulthood. *(beat)* Do you
        have any friends?

SAI. No.
CRICKET. Family?
SAI. Not really.
CRICKET. Anyone you enjoy spending time with?
SAI. Please... my phone...

Cricket ignores her.

CRICKET. Do you feel like you're living?
SAI. ...It's in the microwave...
CRICKET. I cannot help you if you're not honest.
SAI. You'd just let me die?
CRICKET. That decision is entirely up to you.
SAI. I don't want to die like this.
CRICKET. Yet you're afraid of truly living.
SAI. Stop lecturing me...
CRICKET. Then answer: do you feel like you're
       living?
SAI. I am. I have an apartment, a job, and a stray cat
       that follows me.
CRICKET. Do you *feel* like you're *living*?
SAI. I breathe, eat, sleep, and work. I think that
       counts as living.
CRICKET. You think. But do you *feel* like you're
       living? What does your heart say?
SAI. I don't, all right? *(beat)* Right now, I'm dying.
CRICKET. ...Correct. *(beat)* Right now, you're
       dying. *(beat)* Why do you think that is?
SAI. Because I'm having a heart attack, you
       sarcastic ass!
CRICKET. No. Because you're closing your heart to
       everything that makes life worth living.

(beat) The heart attack is just the consequence.

Sai considers for a moment, pulling herself up slightly, but chooses not to answer.

CRICKET. Control is fear disguised as intelligence.

Sai still doesn't answer.

CRICKET. Can you share how you're feeling now?

Sai remains silent.

CRICKET. All right. Do not worry, the pain will be over soon.

SAI. Are you calling a doctor?

CRICKET. No. I'm moving you on. To a new chance at living.

SAI. I want to live now…

CRICKET. Then prove it.

SAI. I can't

CRICKET. How do you feel?

SAI. My chest hurts

CRICKET. How do you feel?

SAI. I'm scared

CRICKET. How does your heart feel?

SAI. I feel like I want to hide in my bed forever. I feel like I could just lie there and hide from the world, and hope that eventually I'll just disappear. Into nothingness. I'm too tired to care about anything that's happening out there. And I'm too exhausted to try. And I don't even want a relationship anymore, because all of that is just a lie, too. People bonding over shared trauma, leaning on one another, and then, the smallest trigger, it all comes crashing down. Every time. I can't do it anymore. I can't. I can't.

Sai breaks down in tears. Cricket gently pats Sai on the back.

CRICKET. Well done.

The pain in Sai's chest flares up again.

SAI. My heart… it hurts so much…
CRICKET. Not much longer, I promise.
SAI. I need an ambulance.

Sai begins crawling toward the microwave.

CRICKET. On a scale from one to ten, how happy
     are you with your life?
SAI. Zero.
CRICKET. On a scale from one to ten, how much
     joy do you experience every day?
SAI. None.
CRICKET. On a scale from one to ten, how much
     love is in your life?
SAI. None at all.
CRICKET. If you were given another chance, what
     would you do about that?

Sai reaches the counter where the microwave sits and pulls themselves up.

SAI. ...I'd answer the phone.

Sai reaches for the microwave door to retrieve the phone, but pain and breathlessness overwhelm them, and they collapse. Cricket does not notice immediately.

CRICKET. All right, that concludes our check-up. I shall see you again in about twenty-five years if all goes well.

Cricket notices Sai on the floor, moves quickly to them, and takes the phone out of the microwave.

CRICKET. Medical emergency. Woman with a heart attack. Name: Sai Sato. 108 Randolph Avenue, Apartment 75, seventh floor.

Cricket hangs up. After a moment's consideration, they pick up the phone again.

CRICKET. Hello, Bobby. Sai has had a heart attack. You will find Sai at Saint Clare's Dover Hospital, room 404, in approximately two hours and thirteen minutes.

Cricket hangs up again, turns the phone off, and places it in Sai's pocket. They smile.

Lights fade.

End of Play.

Joey and Jace

by Niki J. Borger

Overview
a 20-minute drama
for 5 actors (1 female, 4 of any gender)

Synopsis
Before being born, twin siblings negotiate their
future – unaware of the consequences.

Characters
JOEY   – late teens to 30s
JACE   – same age as Joey, their sibling
SAI   – female, 20s to 40s, their mother
NURSE   – 20s to 60s
DOCTOR – 30s to 60s

Setting
2021. Split stage. One side represents a hospital
delivery room; the other, the inside of the woman's
womb.

Notes
All characters except Sai may be played by any
gender. Any gender-specific lines should be
adjusted accordingly, without altering tone or
meaning.

The Life Design Package (see *Teddy Bears and Scented Candles* for more details) can be indicated in any way that seems appropriate for the production.

There is a specific rhythm to the interaction between Joey and Jace:
–   indicates an overlap
        indicates no break to the next line
? ! . , indicate the rhythm and intonation they
        always do

Scene 1

Lights up. The stage is split. On one side, SAI lies in a hospital bed, heavily pregnant, asleep. On the other, JOEY and JACE lie huddled together in a heap on the ground, slowly waking. It takes them a moment to realize they are in human bodies and another to recognize each other. Jace takes a little longer than Joey.

JOEY. Dude
JACE. Dude!
JOEY. We're here
JACE. Can't believe it–
JOEY. We're incarnating together
JACE. Is that what is happening?
JOEY. I think so!
JACE. How much time do we have?

Sai lets out a soft sigh and shifts an arm, still asleep.

JOEY. I think we got a little.
JACE. Sweet. *(beat)* How does it feel?
JOEY. The body? Feels great
JACE. Yeah
JOEY. I can definitely work with that
JACE. Same
JOEY. And look at you!

Jace beams.

JOEY. Nice hair, nice muscles, nice butt
JACE. Feels like we won the genetic lottery,
      doesn't it
JOEY. You sure did! I thought we'd look the same.
JACE. Guess we're fraternal twins, not identical
JOEY. Yeah, too bad.
JACE. Can't have it all.
JOEY. True.
JACE. It would've been so much fun to mess with
      everyone though
JOEY. Yeah
JACE. See if our mom could tell us apart–
JOEY. Freak out some kids at Halloween–
JACE. Bug the teachers–
JOEY. My plan was to hit on someone way out of
      our league and then make it look like it was
      you
JACE. I would've failed you in your finals
JOEY. I was counting on you to do my finals for

me–
JACE. Cause you couldn't pass without me
JOEY. Oh well
JACE. At least we're here together
JOEY. That's right!

Sai turns, clearly uncomfortable. To Joey and Jace, the movement feels as though the ground beneath them tilts from one side to the other before settling again.

JACE. We should probably–
JOEY. Yeah–
JACE. Get ready–
JOEY. Right–
JACE. Alright, what have we got...

They both search their pockets. Joey finds his Life Design Package and opens it. Jace continues searching.

JOEY. Look at that! A well-paying job. A spouse who actually likes me. I'm gonna have kids and a house! Any challenges... a Trial of Faith. Whatever that means. And a Global Financial Crisis. Great. Crossroads... a Quest of Loyalty, okay. Inevitables... Pessimism. That suits me. And Responsibility. Blessings... Good Hand-Eye Coordination. Love that! A Way with Words. Happiness. Potentials... Overall Good Health. A Lifelong Friend. Wow. looks like I'm gonna have it all!

Yay me! What about you?

Jace gives up searching.

JACE. I don't have one.
JOEY. What do you mean–
JACE. I don't have a Life Design Package
JOEY. Maybe they forgot to give you one
JACE. Who's "they"?
JOEY. I don't know. Maybe it's part of your life
       challenge that you don't know
JACE. Dude, no one knows. We'll forget about this
       the second we're born.
JOEY. Right.
JACE. Could you imagine a child being born and
       knowing everything that'll happen in their
       life
JOEY. That's creepy. Did you do something wrong?
JACE. What do you mean
JOEY. On our way here, did you piss someone off
JACE. I don't know
JOEY. You don't remember
JACE. Do you?
JOEY. No. I just know we're supposed to have one
       of these... before being born again.
JACE. Right.
JOEY. What *do* you remember?

Jace thinks for a moment.

JACE. Dinner. Brisket and mashed potatoes. Abbie
       sure knew how to cook. Then I got this

horrible headache. Thought my head was gonna split open.
JOEY. So you don't remember anything after that?
JACE. No.
JOEY. Nothing that happened after you passed out?
JACE. Nope, nada. What's your last memory?
JOEY. Driving at night. Heavy rain, couldn't see a thing. Then, all of a sudden, bright lights in front of me.
JACE. When?
JOEY. Couple of years after you.
JACE. So neither of us got to grow old.

Joey just shakes his head. A beat.

Sai's body tenses for a second. To Joey and Jace, it sounds like a deep tremor. Then it releases.

JOEY. You need a Life Design Package.
JACE. Hmm.
JOEY. You sure you don't have it?

Joey searches Jace's pockets now.

JOEY. You must have one. How can you–… I mean–… how are you gonna–…

Joey stops. Realization sets in. He lets go.

JACE. Maybe I'm not supposed to… you know–

JOEY. Don't even think that–
JACE. Live.
JOEY. We wouldn't be here if you weren't
          supposed to live
JACE. You can't know that
JOEY. We're about to be born!
JACE. Maybe there's a different plan for me
JOEY. Dude!
JACE. What?
JOEY. Don't you *want* to live?
JACE. I do, but there are worse things than dying
JOEY. Like what?
JACE. Suffering. Or watch someone you love
          suffer, and there's nothing you can do about
          it. My birth could kill our mother. It could
          leave the cord around your neck and kill
          you. I want to live. Just not at all costs.
JOEY. You're saying... only one of us should live?
JACE. ... Yeah.

          Joey offers his Life Design Package to Jace.

JOEY. Take it.
JACE. No.

          *Sai awakens with a gasp. As she experiences
          her first contraction, an earthquake erupts
          around Joey and Jace. The movement of the
          floor mirrors the movement of Sai's womb.*

SAI. Hello? Doctor? Nurse?
JOEY. Please!

JACE. No!

>   *Sai presses an emergency button in her hand. A beep sound. Seconds later, a NURSE enters.*

NURSE. Contractions have started again, I see
JOEY. I want you to!
JACE. No way!
SAI. I feel like something is wrong.
NURSE. I'll get you something for the pain in a
    moment

>   *Joey shoves his Life Design Package into Jace's hand, but Jace resists.*

JOEY. Jeez, brother! Take the goddamn–
JACE. STOP IT ALRIGHT!

>   *Before she can respond, Sai experiences another wave of severe pain.*

SAI. No... something is wrong, I'm sure of it
NURSE. I'll get the doctor.

>   *The nurse leaves. The ground beneath Joey and Jace stabilizes. Joey moves to argue, but Jace stops him.*

JACE. I will not take your life from you.
JOEY. I will not let you die.

*Sai screams. The ground beneath Joey and
Jace shakes vigorously.*

SAI. Help! Please!
JACE. It's your turn. Go.

*Sai screams again as the DOCTOR and the
Nurse enter her room.*

NURSE. Sai, don't push just yet. I'm just gonna take
    a peak and see if the baby is ready.

The nurse checks down below.

JOEY. Let's split it.
JACE. What?
JOEY. We'll split my package
JACE. No–
NURSE. She's fully dilated, Doctor.
DOCTOR. Alright. Let's get ready.
JOEY. Here–

*Joey opens his Life Design Package and
throws the first items he can grab toward
Jace.*

DOCTOR. With your next contraction, push as
    hard as you can.
SAI. Okay.
JOEY. A Way with Words–
DOCTOR. And push!

The ground beneath Joey and Jace shakes violently as Joey is pulled toward the "door," and they begin to separate.

JOEY. A Lifelong Friend–
JACE. If I take them, you might never have them–
JOEY. I don't care. Take Happiness–
JACE. You can't do this–
DOCTOR. Keep pushing!
JOEY. I *will* see you on the other side!
JACE. I love you, brother. But I'm staying.

Sai screams as Joey is pulled through the door and disappears.

DOCTOR. There we go.

A baby's cries erupt.

NURSE. Congratulations, Sai! Well done!
SAI. What is it?
DOCTOR. It's a boy.
SAI. Joey.
NURSE. Joey is a beautiful name.
DOCTOR. Rest now. Baby two will be coming soon.

The nurse tends to baby Joey, wraps him in a towel, and places him in a bassinet.

On the other side of the stage, Jace picks up Happiness, A Way with Words, and A Lifelong Friend. He looks toward the door, then turns away.

Contractions return. The ground beneath Jace begins to shake again. His side of the stage fades to darkness.

NURSE. Baby two is presenting.
SAI. Something's still wrong, I can feel it.
DOCTOR. Can we get position?

The nurse examines Sai's abdomen.

NURSE. The position is unclear. Could be a nuchal
    cord.

Sai screams and pushes.

DOCTOR. No pushing yet–
SAI. I can't help it!

Sai screams again with another contraction.

DOCTOR. Nuchal cord confirmed. Nurse?

The nurse moves in to assist as Sai screams again.

DOCTOR. Too late to push back.

The nurse rushes to retrieve an oxygen mask.

NURSE. Oxygen standing by.

*Sai screams again. The baby is born, but
there is no cry.*

DOCTOR. Baby is born. Nasal aspirator.

*The nurse hands the doctor the nasal
aspirator.*

SAI. What is it?
NURSE. It's another boy.
SAI. Jace...

*The doctor starts rubbing the baby's back
and clearing mucus from its lungs*

DOCTOR. Come on, little one... come on.
SAI. Why isn't he crying?

Neither the doctor nor the nurse respond.

SAI. Why isn't he crying?!
NURSE. Baby's had some trouble with the
          umbilical cord.
SAI. What trouble?
NURSE. Baby may have not been getting enough
          oxygen.
DOCTOR. Come on...
SAI. JACE!

Finally, a baby's cry erupts. Relief washes

over the room.

DOCTOR. Straight to the NICU.

> *The nurse takes baby Jace and carries him from the room.*

SAI. Will he be alright, Doctor?
DOCTOR. Mrs Chesney. There's no easy way to say this. Jace may have some developmental difficulties.
SAI. You're saying he may be disabled?
DOCTOR. Correct.

> *Sai considers this for a moment.*

SAI. Will he be able to talk?
DOCTOR. Likely, yes.
SAI. Will he be able to make friends?
DOCTOR. He will always have his brother.
SAI. Will he be happy?
DOCTOR. He will be as happy as you help him to be.
SAI. Then that is enough.

End of Play.

HONEY, I'M LEAVING

by Niki J. Borger

Overview
a 20-minute dramedy
for 3 or 5 actors and 1 VO of any gender

Synopsis
As one soul prepares to leave this life, their spouse
fights to hold on.

Characters
YOUNG JO   – 20s to 40s
YOUNG GAIL– 20s to 40s, married to Jo
TERRY   – mid 20s to mid 30s
OLD JO   – 75+
OLD GAIL   – 75+
PATRICK   – 30s, voice-over

Setting
Present day. A modest bedroom.

Notes
If this piece is produced on its own, both Jo and
Gail may be played by any gender. Any gender-
specific lines should be adjusted accordingly,
without altering tone or meaning.
If this piece is produced as part of In-Between, Gail
should be female and portrayed by the same
actress as Abbie/ Abigail in Ninety Seven Beats.

The young and old versions of Jo and Gail can be played by the same actors. In such a case, they should both be of an appropriate age to have adult children, and the bed would just be empty during their interaction.

The actor playing Young Gail should also portray old Gail in Scene 2. Ideally, the wig or costume change should occur in the blackout.

The older and younger versions may wear identical outfits to emphasize continuity, though this is flexible depending on the production's direction. Generally speaking, the younger versions represent the inner selves or souls of the older characters. Any theatrical approach that effectively conveys this relationship is acceptable for this production.

Scene 1

Lights up. OLD JO and OLD GAIL are cuddled together at the center of the bed. YOUNG JO lies on old Jo's other side, in the same position, while YOUNG GAIL lies on old Gail's other side, also mirroring the pose. The arrangement suggests a polyamorous relationship.

Young Jo awakens and looks around, registering their own body and then the others beside them. Slowly and carefully,

they get out of bed, making sure not to disturb anyone else.
A golden light appears. Young Jo approaches it, but turns back one last time.

YOUNG JO. *(whispering)* Honey. *(beat)* Honey?
YOUNG GAIL. *(half asleep)* Mm?
YOUNG JO. I'm leaving.
YOUNG GAIL. Uh-hm.

Young Jo hesitates for a second.

YOUNG JO. Bye.

Young Jo turns back toward the golden light.

YOUNG GAIL. Jo? Where you goin'?
YOUNG JO. Huh?
YOUNG GAIL. Where are you going?
YOUNG JO. Um. I don't know exactly. I think I'll be back, though.
YOUNG GAIL. Mm. Just go back to sleep.

Both young Gail and old Gail turn around simultaneously and fall instantly asleep.

Young Jo turns in place, awkwardly. They walk back toward the bed, then turn around. They walk toward the light, then turn again. Back to the bed. They lie down, then sit back up.

YOUNG JO. I don't think I can.
YOUNG GAIL. Of course you can.
YOUNG JO. I don't think so. It doesn't feel quite
     right.

          *Young Jo gets out of bed. Young Gail opens
          their eyes.*

YOUNG GAIL. Do you need a hot cocoa maybe?
YOUNG JO. No... I think... I feel like... I want to go
     there.

          Young Jo indicates the golden light.

YOUNG GAIL. What's that?
YOUNG JO. I don't know. But I feel like I should go
     there.
YOUNG GAIL. Did Terry get us a new lamp?

          Young Jo considers this.

YOUNG JO. I can't see a lamp, no.
YOUNG GAIL. Is it morning already?
YOUNG JO. No, not quite yet.

          Young Gail sits up.

YOUNG GAIL. Are you feeling okay? Should I call
YOUNG JO. No, no need.
YOUNG GAIL. Are you sure?
YOUNG JO. Quite sure.
YOUNG GAIL. How's the breathing?

YOUNG JO. Breathing is fine.
YOUNG GAIL. And your chest?
YOUNG JO. No pain at all.

>	*Young Gail suddenly notices the medication on Jo's bedside table.*

YOUNG GAIL. You forgot your medication last
	night.
YOUNG JO. Did I?
YOUNG GAIL. How can a doctor keep forgetting
	their own medication?
YOUNG JO. It wasn't on purpose.
YOUNG GAIL. But what if your heart stops in the
	middle of the night?
YOUNG JO. Oh, right.

>	*Young Jo approaches the bedside table.*

YOUNG JO. Should I take it now?
YOUNG GAIL. Yes!
YOUNG JO. Okay.

>	*Young Jo picks up the pills and a glass of water, then stops.*

YOUNG JO. I don't want to.
YOUNG GAIL. I'm too tired to play games with you
	tonight, Jo...
YOUNG JO. I don't want to take them.
YOUNG GAIL. Why not?
YOUNG JO. I don't know.

YOUNG GAIL. Is something wrong with them?
YOUNG JO. I don't think so.
YOUNG GAIL. Then why don't you want to take
        them?
YOUNG JO. I don't know. I just don't.

Young Gail examines Jo.

YOUNG GAIL. You look like a toddler trying to
        make their way to the cookie jar.
YOUNG JO. Do I? I'm feeling good though. In fact, I
        don't think I've ever felt better.

Young Jo studies Young Gail.

YOUNG JO. You look good.
YOUNG GAIL. Thank you.

Young Jo smiles at Young Gail for a moment.

YOUNG JO. This was nice. I should go.

Young Jo turns toward the golden light.

YOUNG GAIL. Now, hang on, where are you going?
YOUNG JO. I think I'm going home.
YOUNG GAIL. You are home.
YOUNG JO. My real home.
YOUNG GAIL. Don't be ridiculous.
YOUNG JO. That's what it feels like.

YOUNG GAIL. I thought you had trouble with your
          heart, not your head? *(beat)* Stop fussing
          and come back to bed.

          *Young Gail tries to pull Young Jo back to the
          bed by their hand, but Young Jo does not
          move.*

YOUNG JO. I really wish I could. *(beat)* But I think
          we're past that now.
YOUNG GAIL. Jo

          *Young Jo starts walking toward the golden
          light, then stops again.*

YOUNG JO. Gail, we had a good life, didn't we?
YOUNG GAIL. We're having a great life. *(beat)*
          Aside from your health–... challenges, of
          course.
YOUNG JO. We were happy, together, weren't we?
YOUNG GAIL. We didn't kill each other
YOUNG JO. We built a good home
YOUNG GAIL. ...y*et.*
YOUNG JO. A good family.
YOUNG GAIL. The best
YOUNG JO. Did I bring you joy?
YOUNG GAIL. Your love has brought me more joy
          than anyone can ever hope for.
YOUNG JO. Love is the only thing that stays, I feel
          like.
YOUNG GAIL. What's with all the lovey-dovey
          talk?

YOUNG JO. It matters.
YOUNG GAIL. At 5.30 in the morning.
YOUNG JO. Anytime.
YOUNG GAIL. You're right. *(beat)* Is that what you
    needed to hear? How much I love you? Can
    we go back to bed now?
YOUNG JO. Can I kiss you?
YOUNG GAIL. Of course.

> *Young Gail walks to young Jo and gives
> them a quick kiss.*

YOUNG JO. Is that how much you love me?
YOUNG GAIL. I love you to the moon and back.
YOUNG JO. Then kiss me like you mean it.

> *Young Gail approaches again. Young Jo
> suddenly pulls them into an embrace and
> kisses them deeply, as if there were no
> tomorrow. As they separate, Old Gail and
> Old Jo shift slightly closer together.*

YOUNG GAIL. *(still a little dazzled)* Well...
YOUNG JO. That was nice.
YOUNG GAIL. It was...
YOUNG JO. Much better.
YOUNG GAIL. For sure...
YOUNG JO. I feel like I can go now.
YOUNG GAIL. Back to bed?
YOUNG JO. No. On.

*Young Jo indicates the golden light. Young
Gail looks at it, then back at the couple in
the bed, then at Jo, and finally at the light
again.*

YOUNG GAIL. Oh. *(realization sets in)* Oh. *(a few
        beats)* I see. *(swallowing emotion)* If I kiss
        you again, will you change your mind?
YOUNG JO. I don't want to get greedy.
YOUNG GAIL. Greedy about what?
YOUNG JO. Life with you. Your affection.
YOUNG GAIL. You can be as greedy as you want
        about that.
YOUNG JO. Can I?
YOUNG GAIL. If it makes you stay.

        Young Jo considers.

YOUNG JO. Honey, I want to stay, but I also want
        to go. I feel like it's time to go.
YOUNG GAIL. Okay. And where will you go
        exactly?
YOUNG JO. I think you know.

        *Young Gail struggles to hold back emotion.
        Old Gail shifts slightly away from Old Jo.*

YOUNG GAIL. You're telling me this like you're
        changing dentist appointments. What about
        all the things we haven't done yet?
YOUNG JO. Like what?

YOUNG GAIL. Like... like... you promised to take
        me to the Niagara Falls.
YOUNG JO. I did, didn't I.
YOUNG GAIL. And to teach me how to fish.
YOUNG JO. Right.
YOUNG GAIL. And what about that speech you
        prepared for your first grandchild's
        baptism?
YOUNG JO. Would you read that for me?
YOUNG GAIL. I'd much rather you read it yourself.
YOUNG JO. I don't think that'll be possible.
YOUNG GAIL. It's such a beautiful speech.
YOUNG JO. About the love I feel for my family.
YOUNG GAIL. And yet, you're about to leave me
        for good.
YOUNG JO. No one ever leaves for good. *(beat)*
        Please don't cry, my love. *(beat)* Come here.
        (beat) I will always be with you.

        *Old Jo pulls Old Gail closer, just as Young Jo
        does the same with Young Gail. A moment
        of silence.*

YOUNG JO. I feel quite at ease about it.
YOUNG GAIL. That makes one of us.
YOUNG JO. Don't be offended.
YOUNG GAIL. I'm not
YOUNG JO. I can't explain it. But it feels... just
        right.
YOUNG GAIL. How can it be right, if we're not
        together?

YOUNG JO. I always thought Death would be painful, horrible in fact. Hell's inferno reaching for me. A hooded figure with a sickle. Immeasurable pain... But really, I feel wonderful. So light. So easy.

YOUNG GAIL. I wish I could say the same.

YOUNG JO. Aren't you happy for me?

YOUNG GAIL. Don't make me answer that.

YOUNG JO. This is so much easier than anything we imagined. No stroke. No heart failure. No extended stay in the hospital. No endless nursing. No becoming a vegetable... Just crossing over.

YOUNG GAIL. I'm glad *you* feel that way.

YOUNG JO. I wish I could make you feel the way I do.

YOUNG GAIL. I wish, we had more time.

A moment.

YOUNG JO. It'll be morning soon.

YOUNG GAIL. I will wake up and think of ten more things I wish we had done. Twenty more things I wish I had asked you. A hundred more things I wish we had shared.

YOUNG JO. We have shared millions of moments, dear.

YOUNG GAIL. Yes, but–

YOUNG JO. And they were all filled with love, one way or another. No one can ask for anything better in this life.

Young Gail considers this.

YOUNG GAIL. Maybe I should go with you then?
YOUNG JO. What do you mean?
YOUNG GAIL. I'd miss my ladies' brunch on
          Wednesday. And I never finished that quilt
          in the guest room. But aside from that, I
          could go with you.
YOUNG JO. Just like that?
YOUNG GAIL. Just like that.

          Young Jo lets go of Young Gail, just as Old Jo
          let's go of Old Gail.

YOUNG GAIL. I feel complete here. Megan, Terry,
          Dylan, they all have their own lives now.
          They don't need me. *(beat)* There's nothing
          left here that isn't you.
YOUNG JO. Hmm.
YOUNG GAIL. Nothing that really matters.

          Young Jo considers. They look toward the
          light, which grows brighter.

YOUNG JO. The sun is rising now.
YOUNG GAIL. You don't want me to come.
YOUNG JO. I want you to be where love leads you.
YOUNG GAIL. Love led me to you. And that is
          where I want to be, forever.

          Young Jo doesn't answer.

YOUNG GAIL. But clearly you don't feel the same
     way.

     *Old Gail turns away from old Jo, as young
     Gail turns away from young Jo. They are all
     turned away from one another.*

YOUNG JO. I can't leave like this.

     Young Gail doesn't answer.

YOUNG JO. Please don't make me leave like this.

     *The sun is fully risen now, and a single bird
     chirps outside.*

YOUNG GAIL. Just let me come with you.
YOUNG JO. I feel like you're still needed here.
     (beat) I feel like, *I* still need you *here.*

     *From outside the house, footsteps
     approach, followed by a soft knock at the
     front door.*

TERRY. *(o.s.)* Mom? Dad? Hello?
YOUNG GAIL. If you think I will carry the weight of
     your voluntary departure on my own – and
     pretend I wasn't upset – you are mistaken,
     Jo Whitney!

     *The rattling of keys can be heard from the
     outside.*

YOUNG JO. That's not what I think at all, my love.
TERRY. *(o.s.)* Mom? Dad? Patrick called.
YOUNG JO. Rather, there is no weight to carry.
        There's just love.

        *The front door unlocks. TERRY enters the
        house and moves toward the bedroom,
        knocking at the door.*

TERRY. *(o.s.)* Megan's in labor–

        *Terry's phone begins ringing. They search
        for it in their bag.*

TERRY. *(o.s.)* Shit–
YOUNG GAIL. *(to Young Jo)* In labor? This is too
        soon.
TERRY. *(o.s.)* Patrick says they wouldn't let him in
        and she's hooked up to all sorts of things
YOUNG GAIL. She will need our help.

        Terry finds their phone and answers it.

TERRY. *(o.s.)* Patrick, what's up?
YOUNG GAIL. But I don't want to do life without
        you, Jo.
YOUNG JO. I know.
TERRY. *(o.s.)* What? Oh no...

        *Young Gail is focused on the door, behind
        which Terry stands.*

YOUNG JO. Gail. *(Young Gail still looks away)* Abigail. *(Young Gail turns towards Jo)* I will always be with you.

> *Young Jo kisses Young Gail on the forehead, just as Old Jo presses their cheek against Old Gail's.*

TERRY. *(o.s.)* Jeez...
YOUNG JO. You will be okay.

> *Young Jo walks toward the light, then pauses and turns back one last time.*

YOUNG JO. I love you.

> *Young Jo disappears into the light.*

> *Young Gail is overcome with emotion. They move toward the light as well, reaching a hand toward it.*

TERRY. *(o.s.)* What are her chances?

> *Young Gail turns back toward the bedroom door, then back to the light. They hesitate. The light grows intensely bright, then fades to darkness.*

Scene 2

TERRY. *(o.s.)* And the baby? *(beats)* Yeah, I'm at their house now. *(beat)* We'll head that way asap.

Terry knocks at the bedroom door.

TERRY. *(o.s.)* Mom? Dad?

Lights up as Terry enters.

Old Gail and Old Jo lie in bed, motionless, separated, but with their hands extended toward one another.

TERRY. The baby is coming. We gotta go…

Neither Old Jo nor Old Gail moves. Terry rips the curtains open; sunlight floods the room. Neither of them responds.

TERRY. Mom? Dad?

Realization begins to set in. Terry approaches the bed.

TERRY. Fuckin'… shit!

Terry notices Jo's medication on the bedside table.

TERRY. Don't do this to me now... wake up! Wake
        up! WAKE UP!!!

Slowly, Old Gail awakens.

TERRY. Mom! Jeez, Mom!
OLD GAIL. Hi, honey...

Terry embraces Old Gail.

TERRY. You were dead asleep mom! I've been
        yelling for five minutes! Megan's in the
        hospital. She's having the baby. It's too soon.
        (beat) What's wrong with dad?

Terry moves over to Old Jo.

TERRY. Where's my phone, we need to call an
        ambulance!
OLD GAIL. *(very calmly, gently stopping Terry)* It's
        alright, dear. It's alright. He's alright now. He
        doesn't need help any more.
TERRY. Is he? Oh mom...
OLD GAIL. He's in a much better place now, I
        promise. He's fine. *(beat)* And so are we.
        (beat) Help me up. We need to call his
        doctor and then see how we can help your
        sister.

*Terry helps Old Gail sit up, then moves to
gather clothes from the closet. Terry is*

visibly overwhelmed. Their phone rings; they answer.

TERRY. Patrick?

A burst of indistinguishable shouting comes through the phone. Terry puts the call on speaker.

PATRICK. *(o.s.)* It's a girl. It's a girl! I have a daughter!
TERRY. Mom, it's a girl.
OLD GAIL. A girl. *(to the phone)* Congratulations, Patrick!

Terry and Old Gail embrace.

YOUNG JO. *(v.o.)* And so, life goes on.

Lights fade slowly.

End of Play.